AI PRODUCT MANAGEMENT

A PRACTICAL GUIDE FOR BUILDING, LAUNCHING, AND SCALING AI PRODUCTS

KUMAR VISHWESH

Made with ♥ on the Notion Press Platform
www.notionpress.com

Contents

Contents

Preface

Artificial intelligence (AI) is revolutionizing the way we do business, and AI product management is at the forefront of this transformation. In this practical guide, you'll learn the skills and strategies needed to successfully develop, launch, and scale AI products. We'll start by introducing you to the role of an AI product manager and the importance of AI in today's business landscape. From there, you'll learn how to understand the AI ecosystem and identify the right use cases for your AI product. You'll also discover how to build and manage an interdisciplinary team, design and develop an AI product, and launch and market it effectively. Throughout the book, you'll find real-world examples and best practices for growing and scaling your AI product. Whether you're a product manager, engineer, data scientist, or entrepreneur, this book will provide you with the knowledge and tools you need to succeed in the exciting field of AI product management.

Key topics covered include:

Understanding the AI landscape and key players

Developing an AI product roadmap

Building and managing an AI product team

Designing and developing an AI product

Launching and marketing an AI product Growing and scaling an AI product

* * *

Introduction to AI product management

CHAPTER ONE

Defining AI product management

AI product management is the process of overseeing the development and deployment of AI-powered products. This includes determining the strategy, roadmap, and goals for the product, as well as coordinating with cross-functional teams to ensure that the product meets the needs of the target market. AI product managers must have a strong understanding of both business and technical concepts, as they must be able to translate customer needs into technical requirements and work with engineers to bring the product to life. They must also be able to effectively communicate the value of the product to stakeholders and customers.

* * *

What is AI Product Management?

AI product management involves overseeing the development and deployment of AI-powered products. This includes defining the product strategy and roadmap, gathering and analyzing customer feedback, collaborating with cross-functional teams, and setting and tracking key performance indicators (KPIs) to measure the success of the product.

* * *

Key Responsibilities of an AI Product Manager

Some of the key responsibilities of an AI product manager include: Defining the strategy and roadmap for the AI product Identifying and prioritizing customer needs and pain points Collaborating with cross-functional teams to design and develop the AI product Gathering and analyzing customer feedback to inform product decisions Setting and tracking key performance indicators (KPIs) to measure the success of the AI product Communicating the value of the AI product to stakeholders and customers

* * *

Skills and Competencies for AI Product Management

To be effective in their role, AI product managers should have the following skills and competencies: **Business Acumen:** The ability to understand and analyze market trends, customer needs, and financial data to inform product decisions.

Technical knowledge: A strong understanding of AI technologies and how they can be applied to solve business problems.

Communication and collaboration: The ability to effectively communicate with cross-functional teams and stakeholders, as well as facilitate collaboration among team members.

Strategic thinking: The ability to develop long-term plans and goals for the AI product and align them with the overall business strategy.

Data analysis: The ability to analyze data to inform product decisions and track the success of the AI product.

* * *

Challenges of AI Product Management

AI product management can be a complex and challenging role, as it involves coordinating the development and deployment of a highly technical product in a rapidly evolving market.

Some of the specific challenges that AI product managers may face include:

Managing the trade-offs between short-term and long-term goals

Balancing the need for innovation with the need for stability and reliability

Dealing with the uncertainty and complexity inherent in developing and deploying AI products

Managing the expectations of stakeholders and customers

Ensuring that the AI product is ethically and socially responsible.

* * *

Conclusion

Overall, AI product management involves coordinating the development and deployment of AI-powered products in a way that meets the needs of the target market and aligns with the overall business strategy. It requires a strong understanding of both business and technical concepts, as well as the ability to effectively communicate with cross-functional teams and stakeholders.

* * *

CHAPTER TWO

The role of an AI product manager

The role of an AI product manager is to ensure that the AI product meets the needs of the target market and aligns with the overall business strategy. This involves defining the product strategy and roadmap, gathering and analyzing customer feedback, collaborating with cross-functional teams, and setting and tracking key performance indicators (KPIs) to measure the success of the product. AI product managers must also be able to effectively communicate the value of the product to stakeholders and customers. They should have a strong understanding of both business and technical concepts, as well as the ability to analyze data and make informed decisions.

* * *

Examples of AI Product Managers

The role of an AI product manager is to oversee the development and launch of AI-based products, from ideation to release. They are responsible for understanding customer needs, working with cross-functional teams to develop product requirements, ensuring product quality, and ultimately driving revenue growth.

Some of the examples of AI Product Managers are listed below:

1. Product manager for Amazon's Alexa
2. Product manager for Google's machine learning platform, TensorFlow
3. Product manager for a healthcare AI startup that is focused on developing an AI-powered diagnostic tool

Let's deep-dive into each.

* * *

Product manager for Amazon's Alexa

One example of an AI product manager is the product manager for Amazon's Alexa. They are responsible for managing the development and launch of new features for the Alexa ecosystem, as well as driving growth and engagement of the platform. This includes working with teams across Amazon to develop new voice-based capabilities and integrations with third-party services, as well as ensuring that the platform remains reliable and secure. The Alexa product manager must also stay up-to-date on the latest AI and machine learning technologies, and understand how they can be applied to enhance the user experience and create new revenue opportunities.

* * *

Product manager for Google's machine learning platform, TensorFlow

Another example of an AI product manager could be the product manager for Google's machine learning platform, TensorFlow. They would be responsible for managing the development and release of new features for the platform, working closely with engineering and research teams to ensure that the platform meets the needs of developers and data scientists. This would include understanding the latest trends and developments in machine learning, and working to incorporate these into the platform. The product manager would also work with sales and marketing teams to drive the adoption of TensorFlow among businesses and organizations, and to create new revenue streams through products and services built on top of the platform. Overall, the role of an AI product manager would be to understand the needs of users and the market, and to lead the development of AI-based products that meet those needs and drive growth for the company.

* * *

Product manager for a healthcare AI startup that is focused on developing an AI-powered diagnostic tool

Another example of an AI product manager could be the product manager for a healthcare AI startup that is focused on developing an AI-powered diagnostic tool. They would be responsible for managing the entire product lifecycle, from ideation to launch and beyond. This would involve working with healthcare professionals and researchers to identify areas where AI could improve diagnosis accuracy and efficiency, and then leading a team of developers and data scientists to build and refine the tool. The product manager would also be responsible for ensuring that the tool meets regulatory requirements and standards, and for working with marketing and sales teams to promote the tool to healthcare providers and organizations. This would require a deep understanding of the healthcare industry and the unique challenges and opportunities that AI can bring to it, as well as the ability to work closely with technical teams to develop and deploy cutting-edge AI technology. Overall, the role of an AI product manager in a healthcare startup would be to create a product that improves patient outcomes and drives growth for the company, while also navigating the complex regulatory landscape of the healthcare industry. * * * Conclusion AI product managers are responsible for making strategic decisions about the use of AI technologies in the product, including selecting appropriate algorithms and models, and integrating them into the product. They must stay up-to-date with the latest AI technologies and ensure that the AI technology performs as expected. To be successful in this role, AI product managers should have strong technical expertise in AI technologies, as well as excellent communication, project management, and data analysis skills

* * *

CHAPTER THREE

The importance of AI in business

AI is rapidly transforming many industries and has the potential to revolutionize how businesses operate. AI-powered products can help businesses automate tasks, make more informed decisions, and improve efficiency.

* * *

Overview of AI in Business

AI is the use of computers and machine learning algorithms to perform tasks that would typically require human intelligence, such as recognizing patterns, making decisions, and learning from experience. AI has the potential to transform many industries, including healthcare, finance, and manufacturing.

* * *

Benefits of AI in Business

Some of the benefits of AI in business include:

Improved decision-making: AI can analyze large amounts of data and identify patterns and trends that would be impossible for humans to detect. This can help businesses make more informed decisions, such as identifying new market opportunities or optimizing marketing campaigns.

Increased efficiency: AI can automate tasks that are repetitive or time-consuming, freeing up employees to focus on more strategic and creative tasks. This can help businesses improve efficiency and reduce costs.

Enhanced customer experience: AI can be used to personalize the customer experience, such as by providing personalized recommendations or automating customer service inquiries.

Increased competitiveness: The adoption of AI can give businesses a competitive edge in their industry by allowing them to leverage the latest technologies to improve their operations.

* * *

Challenges of AI in Business

While AI has the potential to bring many benefits to businesses, there are also challenges to consider.

Some of the challenges of AI in business include:

Integration and adoption: Implementing AI can be a complex and time-consuming process, requiring significant investments in technology and training.

Ethical and social concerns: AI raises ethical and social concerns, such as the potential for job displacement and the need to ensure that AI systems are transparent and accountable.

Regulatory challenges: AI is a rapidly evolving field, and there may be regulatory challenges associated with the adoption of AI technologies.

Talent shortages: There is a shortage of qualified AI professionals, which can make it difficult for businesses to find and hire the talent they need to implement AI projects.

* * *

Conclusion

Overall, the adoption of AI has the potential to greatly impact business operations and drive growth. While there are challenges to consider, the benefits of AI in business make it an important area for businesses to explore. To maximize the potential of AI, it is important for businesses to carefully consider their strategy and approach to implementation, as well as address ethical and social concerns.

* * *

Understanding the AI landscape

CHAPTER FOUR

Types of AI technologies

AI technologies are a broad category of computer systems and machine learning algorithms designed to perform tasks that would typically require human intelligence, such as recognizing patterns, making decisions, and learning from experience. There are several types of AI technologies, each with its own unique capabilities and applications.

* * *

Overview of AI Technologies

AI technologies can be broadly classified into two categories: narrow or general AI. Narrow AI is designed to perform a specific task or set of tasks, while general AI is designed to perform a wide range of tasks.

Within these categories, there are several specific types of AI technologies, including:

Machine learning: Machine learning algorithms use data to learn and improve over time, without being explicitly programmed. There are several types of machine learning, including supervised learning, unsupervised learning, and reinforcement learning.

Natural language processing (NLP): NLP technologies allow computers to understand and process human language. This can be used for tasks such as language translation, sentiment analysis, and chatbot development.

Computer vision: Computer vision technologies allow computers to process and analyze images and videos. This can be used for tasks such as object recognition, facial recognition, and image classification.

Robotics: Robotics technologies involve the use of machines to perform tasks that would normally require human labor. This can include manufacturing, transportation, and healthcare.

* * *

Applications of AI Technologies

AI technologies have a wide range of applications in various industries.

Some examples of the applications of AI technologies include:

Healthcare: AI technologies can be used to analyze medical data to identify trends and patterns, as well as to assist with diagnosis and treatment.

Finance: AI technologies can be used to analyze financial data and identify trends, as well as to automate tasks such as fraud detection and risk assessment.

Manufacturing: AI technologies can be used to automate tasks in manufacturing, such as quality control and supply chain management.

Retail: AI technologies can be used to personalize the customer experience, such as by providing personalized recommendations or automating customer service inquiries.

Transportation: AI technologies can be used to optimize transportation routes and improve safety, such as through the use of self-driving vehicles.

* * *

Future of AI Technologies

AI technologies are rapidly evolving and have the potential to transform many industries.

Some areas where AI technologies are expected to have a significant impact in the future include:

Healthcare: AI technologies are expected to play a larger role in healthcare, such as through the use of AI-powered assistants for diagnosis and treatment.

Education: AI technologies are expected to revolutionize education, such as through the use of personalized learning platforms.

Manufacturing: AI technologies are expected to further automate manufacturing processes, leading to increased efficiency and productivity.

Transportation: AI technologies are expected to play a significant role in the future of transportation, such as through the widespread adoption of self-driving vehicles.

Social impact: AI technologies are expected to have a significant impact on society, raising ethical and social concerns that will need to be addressed.

* * *

Conclusion

AI technologies are a rapidly evolving field with a wide range of applications across various industries. While there are many exciting possibilities for the future of AI, it is important to carefully consider the ethical and social implications of these technologies.

* * *

CHAPTER FIVE

Key players and stakeholders in the AI ecosystem

Artificial intelligence (AI) has become an increasingly important part of the modern world, with applications ranging from self-driving cars to virtual assistants to medical diagnosis. As AI continues to grow and evolve, it is important to understand the key players and stakeholders that make up the AI ecosystem. These include AI researchers and developers, Tech companies, Governments, End users & Ethicists, and policymakers.

* * *

AI researchers and developers

AI researchers and developers are the individuals who create and advance the field of AI. They may work in academia, industry, or government research labs, and are responsible for developing new algorithms, techniques, and applications for AI.

These individuals often have advanced degrees in computer science, mathematics, or related fields and may specialize in areas such as machine learning, natural language processing, or robotics.

* * *

Tech companies

Tech companies are major players in the AI ecosystem, as they often have the resources and expertise to develop and commercialize AI products and services.

These companies may include large multinational corporations, such as Google and Microsoft, as well as smaller startups focused on specific AI-related areas, such as self-driving cars or virtual assistants.

* * *

Governments

Governments around the world are increasingly interested in AI, both as a potential tool for improving services and as an economic opportunity. As a result, governments are often key stakeholders in the AI ecosystem, providing funding for research and development, setting regulations and policies related to AI, and working to ensure that the benefits of AI are distributed fairly.

* * *

End users

End users are individuals and organizations who use AI products and services in their daily lives or business operations.

These may include consumers using virtual assistants or self-driving cars, businesses using AI-powered customer service or marketing tools, or healthcare providers using AI to assist with diagnoses and treatment plans.

* * *

Ethicists and policymakers

As AI becomes more prevalent and powerful, there is a growing concern about its potential impacts on society and the ethical implications of its development and use. Ethicists and policymakers play a critical role in addressing these concerns and ensuring that AI is developed and used in a responsible and ethical manner.

* * *

Conclusion

The AI ecosystem is complex and multifaceted, involving a wide range of players and stakeholders. From AI researchers and developers to tech companies to end users, each group plays an important role in the advancement and impact of AI. As the field continues to evolve, it will be important for all of these stakeholders to work together to ensure that the benefits of AI are realized while minimizing any negative impacts.

* * *

CHAPTER SIX

Understanding the ethical implications of AI

As artificial intelligence (AI) continues to advance and become more prevalent in our daily lives, it is important to consider the ethical implications of its development and use. There are a number of ethical concerns that arise in relation to AI, including Bias and discrimination, Privacy and data protection, Autonomy and control, Unemployment and job displacement & Transparency and accountability.

* * *

Bias and discrimination

AI systems are only as unbiased as the data they are trained on and the algorithms used to analyze that data. If the data used to train an AI system is biased or discriminatory, the resulting AI system may also exhibit these biases. This can have serious consequences, such as the amplification of existing societal inequalities or the exclusion of certain groups from opportunities or services.

* * *

Privacy and data protection

AI systems often rely on large amounts of data to function, including personal data such as names, addresses, and sensitive information like medical records. The collection, storage, and use of this data raise significant privacy and data protection concerns. There is a risk that personal data may be misused or accessed without proper consent, leading to potential harm or abuse.

* * *

Autonomy and control

As AI systems become more advanced and autonomous, there is a risk that they may make decisions that have significant consequences for individuals or society. There is a need for clear and transparent frameworks to govern the decision-making processes of AI systems and ensure that they are accountable for their actions.

* * *

Unemployment and job displacement

AI has the potential to significantly impact the job market, both positively and negatively. On the one hand, AI can automate certain tasks and processes, freeing humans to focus on more complex and creative tasks. On the other hand, there is a risk that AI may displace certain jobs, leading to unemployment or the need for workers to retrain for new roles.

* * *

Transparency and accountability

As AI becomes more prevalent and influential, it is important to ensure that it is transparent and accountable in its decision-making processes. This includes making sure that the algorithms and data used by AI systems are open and transparent, and that there are clear mechanisms in place to hold AI systems accountable for their actions.

* * *

Conclusion

The ethical implications of AI are complex and multifaceted and require careful consideration and ongoing dialogue among stakeholders. Ensuring that AI is developed and used in a responsible and ethical manner will require the efforts of researchers, developers, policymakers, and society as a whole.

* * *

Developing an AI product roadmap

CHAPTER SEVEN

Identifying business objectives and use cases for AI

Artificial intelligence (AI) has the potential to significantly impact businesses of all sizes and industries. However, before implementing AI, it is important for businesses to carefully consider their business objectives and identify the specific use cases where AI can provide the greatest value. Some key steps in this process include: Defining business objectives, Identifying areas where AI can add value, Assessing the feasibility of AI implementation & Developing a roadmap for implementation.

* * *

Define business objectives

The first step in identifying potential use cases for AI is to clearly define the business objectives that the company is trying to achieve. This may include improving efficiency, reducing costs, increasing revenue, or enhancing customer experience. Understanding the specific goals that the company is trying to achieve will help narrow down the potential use cases for AI.

* * *

Identify areas where AI can add value

Once the business objectives have been defined, the next step is to identify the specific areas where AI can add value. This may include analyzing data to identify trends or patterns, automating repetitive tasks, or enhancing customer service through the use of chatbots or virtual assistants.

* * *

Assess the feasibility of AI implementation

Before implementing AI, it is important to assess the feasibility of using AI to achieve the desired business objectives. This may involve considering the availability of data, the complexity of the task, the costs and resources required, and any potential risks or challenges.

* * *

Develop a roadmap for implementation

Once the business objectives and potential use cases for AI have been identified and assessed, the next step is to develop a roadmap for implementation. This may involve creating a timeline, identifying resources and budgets, and establishing clear goals and metrics to measure the success of the AI implementation.

* * *

Examples

Here are some examples of identifying business objectives and use cases for AI:

Customer Service: An objective could be to improve customer service by reducing wait times and improving the accuracy of responses. An AI use case could be to implement a chatbot that can quickly and accurately respond to customer inquiries, freeing up human customer service representatives to handle more complex issues.

Marketing: An objective could be to increase the effectiveness of marketing campaigns by targeting the right audience with the right message. An AI use case could be to develop a recommendation engine that can analyze customer data to predict which products or services they are most likely to be interested in, and then recommend those products or services to them.

Supply Chain Management: An objective could be to optimize the supply chain to reduce costs and improve efficiency. An AI use case could be to implement predictive analytics that can forecast demand for products, allowing businesses to adjust production and inventory levels accordingly, and reduce waste.

Fraud Detection: An objective could be to improve fraud detection and prevention, minimizing financial losses. An AI use case could be to develop an anomaly detection system that can analyze transactions and identify unusual patterns that may indicate fraud.

Healthcare: An objective could be to improve patient outcomes and reduce costs. An AI use case could be to develop a predictive analytics model that can analyze patient data to identify those at risk of developing a particular disease, allowing for early intervention and prevention.

Financial Services: An objective could be to improve the accuracy and speed of credit underwriting. An AI use case could be to develop a credit scoring model that can analyze a wide range of data sources (e.g., credit history, employment history, social media activity) to more accurately predict creditworthiness and reduce the risk of defaults.

E-commerce: An objective could be to improve the customer experience by providing personalized recommendations and improving search functionality. An AI use case could be to develop a product recommendation engine that can analyze customer browsing and purchase history to provide personalized product recommendations, and a natural language processing-based search engine that can better understand customer queries and provide more accurate search results.

Manufacturing: An objective could be to reduce downtime and improve productivity by optimizing equipment maintenance. An AI use case could be to develop a predictive maintenance system that can monitor equipment sensor data to detect anomalies and predict when maintenance is needed, allowing maintenance to be scheduled proactively and reducing the risk of costly equipment failures.

Transportation: An objective could be to improve safety and efficiency in transportation. An AI use case could be to develop a predictive maintenance system for vehicles that can monitor sensor data to detect potential issues and schedule repairs proactively, reducing the risk of accidents and improving overall fleet efficiency.

Human Resources: An objective could be to improve employee retention and satisfaction. An AI use case could be to develop a sentiment analysis tool that can analyze employee feedback (e.g., from surveys or social media) to identify areas where improvements can be made, allowing companies to proactively address employee concerns and improve overall employee satisfaction.

* * *

Conclusion

Identifying business objectives and use cases for AI is a critical step in the process of implementing AI in a business setting. By carefully considering the specific goals that the company is trying to achieve and identifying the areas where AI can add value, businesses can maximize the benefits of AI while minimizing any potential risks or challenges.

* * *

CHAPTER EIGHT

Defining the scope and goals of the AI products

Artificial intelligence (AI) has the potential to revolutionize a wide range of industries and applications, from self-driving cars to virtual assistants to medical diagnosis. However, before developing an AI product, it is important to carefully define the scope and goals of the project to ensure that it is successful and meets the needs of the intended users. Some key considerations in this process include: Identifying the problem or opportunity, Defining the target audience, Setting clear and achievable goals & Defining the scope of the project.

* * *

Identify the problem or opportunity

The first step in defining the scope and goals of an AI product is to identify the problem or opportunity that the product is intended to address. This may involve identifying a specific business need, customer pain point, or technological challenge. Understanding the problem or opportunity that the product is intended to solve will help guide the development process and ensure that the product meets the needs of its users.

* * *

Define the target audience

It is important to carefully consider the target audience for the AI product, as this will influence the scope and goals of the project. This may include identifying the specific demographics, needs, and preferences of the intended users, as well as any potential constraints or limitations that may impact the product's design or functionality.

* * *

Set clear and achievable goals

Once the problem or opportunity and target audience have been identified, the next step is to set clear and achievable goals for the AI product. These goals should be specific, measurable, attainable, relevant, and time-bound (SMART). Setting clear goals will help guide the development process and ensure that the product meets the needs of its users.

* * *

Define the scope of the project

Defining the scope of the project is critical to ensuring that the AI product is successful. This may involve identifying the specific features and functionality that the product will include, as well as any constraints or limitations that may impact the development process. It is important to carefully balance the scope of the project with the available resources and timeline to ensure that the project is feasible and can be completed successfully.

* * *

Examples

Here are some examples of the scope and goals of the AI product:

Virtual Personal Shopping Assistant: The scope of this AI product could be to provide a virtual personal shopping assistant to help customers make informed purchasing decisions. The goal could be to improve customer satisfaction and increase sales by providing personalized recommendations and a seamless shopping experience.

Autonomous Driving System: The scope of this AI product could be to develop an autonomous driving system for vehicles. The goal could be to improve safety, reduce traffic congestion, and provide more efficient transportation options.

Medical Diagnosis Tool: The scope of this AI product could be to develop a medical diagnosis tool that can assist doctors in making more accurate diagnoses. The goal could be to improve patient outcomes by providing faster and more accurate diagnoses.

Fraud Detection System: The scope of this AI product could be to develop a fraud detection system for financial institutions. The goal could be to reduce the risk of financial losses due to fraudulent activities and to improve regulatory compliance.

Customer Service Chatbot: The scope of this AI product could be to develop a customer service chatbot that can handle customer inquiries and provide personalized assistance. The goal could be to reduce customer service wait times and improve customer satisfaction.

Smart Home Automation System: The scope of this AI product could be to develop a smart home automation system that can control various household appliances and devices. The goal could be to improve convenience, energy efficiency, and overall home security.

Language Translation Tool: The scope of this AI product could be to develop a language translation tool that can translate text or speech from one language to another in real-time. The goal could be to improve communication across different languages and cultures.

Personalized News Feed: The scope of this AI product could be to develop a personalized news feed that can deliver relevant news articles to users based on their interests and browsing history. The goal could be to increase user engagement and loyalty by providing a more personalized and relevant experience.

Predictive Maintenance System: The scope of this AI product could be to develop a predictive maintenance system for industrial equipment. The goal could be to reduce maintenance costs and downtime by detecting potential equipment failures before they occur.

Agricultural Yield Optimization Tool: The scope of this AI product could be to develop an agricultural yield optimization tool that can analyze data on soil moisture, weather patterns, and crop growth to provide farmers with personalized recommendations on irrigation, fertilization, and pest control. The goal could be to increase crop yields and reduce waste.

* * *

Conclusion

Defining the scope and goals of an AI product is a critical step in the development process. By carefully considering the problem or opportunity that the product is intended to address, the target audience, and the specific goals and scope of the project, businesses and developers can ensure that the AI product meets the needs of its users and is successful.

* * *

CHAPTER NINE

Creating a high-level roadmap for the AI product

Developing an artificial intelligence (AI) product involves a complex and multifaceted process that requires careful planning and coordination. One key tool that can help guide this process is a high-level roadmap, which outlines the major milestones and goals for the AI product. Some key considerations in creating a high-level roadmap for an AI product include: Define the scope and goals of the AI product, Identify key milestones and deliverables, Establish a timeline & Identify resources and dependencies.

* * *

Define the scope and goals of the AI product

Before creating a roadmap, it is important to clearly define the scope and goals of the AI product. This may involve identifying the specific problem or opportunity that the product is intended to address, the target audience, and the specific features and functionality that the product will include. Understanding the scope and goals of the AI product will help inform the roadmap and ensure that it is focused and achievable.

* * *

Identify key milestones and deliverables

The next step in creating a high-level roadmap is to identify the key milestones and deliverables that will be required to achieve the goals of the AI product. This may include tasks such as data collection and preprocessing, model development and training, testing and validation, and deployment. Identifying these milestones and deliverables will help guide the development process and ensure that the team stays on track.

* * *

Establish a timeline

It is important to establish a timeline for the AI product development process, including the expected duration of each milestone and deliverable. This will help the team stay on track and ensure that the project stays within budget and on schedule.

* * *

Identify resources and dependencies

In order to successfully complete the AI product development process, it is important to identify the resources and dependencies that will be required. This may include human resources, such as data scientists and developers, as well as financial resources, technical resources, and external partners. Understanding the resources and dependencies will help the team plan and allocate resources effectively.

* * *

Examples

Here are some examples of a high-level roadmap for an AI product:

Virtual Personal Shopping Assistant:

1. Conduct market research and identify customer needs and pain points.

2. Develop a minimum viable product (MVP) that can provide basic shopping assistance to customers.

3. Collect feedback from early users and iterate on the MVP.

4. Implement natural language processing and computer vision capabilities to improve the assistant's ability to understand customer requests and preferences.

5. Integrate with e-commerce platforms to provide personalized product recommendations and a seamless shopping experience.

6. Develop a mobile app to enable customers to access the assistant on-the-go.

7. Explore partnerships with retailers and other companies to expand the assistant's capabilities and reach.

Autonomous Driving System:

1. Conduct market research and identify potential use cases and target customers.

2. Develop a simulation environment to test and validate the autonomous driving system.

3. Develop a prototype of the system and conduct field tests under controlled conditions.

4. Collect data on system performance and user feedback and iterate on the prototype.

5. Develop a production-ready version of the system that meets safety and regulatory requirements.

6. Partner with automakers and transportation companies to integrate the system into their vehicles and operations.

7. Explore opportunities to expand the system's capabilities and applications, such as package delivery or public transportation.

Medical Diagnosis Tool:

1. Conduct market research and identify potential use cases and target customers.

2. Develop a dataset of medical images and diagnoses to train the AI model.

3. Develop a prototype of the tool and conduct clinical trials to validate its accuracy and effectiveness.

4. Collect data on tool performance and user feedback and iterate on the prototype.

5. Develop a user-friendly interface that can provide doctors with real-time diagnostic recommendations based on patient data.

6. Partner with hospitals and medical institutions to integrate the tool into their diagnostic workflows.

7. Explore opportunities to expand the tool's capabilities and applications, such as remote diagnosis or telemedicine.

* * *

Conclusion

Creating a high-level roadmap for an AI product is a critical step in the development process. By outlining the major milestones and goals for the product, the team can stay on track and ensure that the product is delivered on time and within budget. A well-designed roadmap can also help identify potential risks or challenges and allow the team to plan accordingly.

* * *

Building an AI product team

CHAPTER TEN

Identifying and hiring the right team members

As businesses and organizations increasingly turn to artificial intelligence (AI) to solve complex problems and drive innovation, it is becoming increasingly important to build strong, talented teams to develop and implement AI solutions. However, finding and hiring the right team members can be a challenge, as AI requires a unique blend of technical skills, business acumen, and problem-solving ability. Some key considerations in identifying and hiring the right team members include: Identify the skills and expertise required, Consider team diversity, Look beyond traditional AI roles & Assess fit with company culture.

* * *

Identify the skills and expertise required

The first step in identifying and hiring the right team members is to identify the specific skills and expertise that will be required to successfully develop and implement the AI solution. This may include technical skills such as machine learning, data science, and programming, as well as domain-specific expertise and business acumen.

* * *

Consider team diversity

Diversity is an important factor to consider when building an AI team, as it can bring a range of perspectives and approaches to problem-solving. This may include diversity in terms of gender, race, ethnicity, and background, as well as diversity in terms of skills and expertise.

* * *

Look beyond traditional AI roles

While AI often requires technical expertise, it is also important to consider hiring team members who bring a range of skills and experiences to the table. This may include individuals with expertise in areas such as project management, design, or communication, who can help ensure that the AI solution is delivered effectively and meets the needs of the end users.

* * *

Assess fit with company culture

It is important to consider not only the skills and expertise of potential team members, but also whether they will be a good fit with the company culture and values. This can help ensure that the team is able to work effectively together and achieve its goals.

* * *

Conclusion

Identifying and hiring the right team members is a critical step in the process of developing and implementing AI solutions. By carefully considering the skills and expertise required, the importance of diversity, the potential value of non-traditional AI roles, and fit with company culture, businesses and organizations can build strong, effective teams that can drive innovation and success.

* * *

CHAPTER ELEVEN

Managing an interdisciplinary team

Artificial intelligence (AI) projects often require teams with a diverse range of skills and expertise, including machine learning, data science, programming, and domain-specific knowledge. This can create challenges in terms of managing an interdisciplinary team, as team members may come from different backgrounds and have different approaches to problem-solving.

Some key considerations in managing an interdisciplinary team include: Clearly define roles and responsibilities, Foster open communication and collaboration, Establish a project management structure & Provide resources and support.

* * *

Clearly define roles and responsibilities

It is important to clearly define the roles and responsibilities of team members, including their specific areas of expertise and their contributions to the project. This can help ensure that everyone understands their role and how it fits into the overall project goals.

* * *

Foster open communication and collaboration

Effective communication and collaboration are critical to the success of any team, and this is especially true for interdisciplinary teams. Encourage team members to share their ideas and approaches, and create an open and inclusive environment where all team members feel comfortable participating.

* * *

Establish a project management structure

Having a clear project management structure in place can help ensure that the team stays organized and on track. This may involve using project management tools and techniques such as agile methodologies or establishing clear goals, timelines, and milestones.

* * *

Provide resources and support

Ensuring that team members have the resources and support they need to succeed is critical to the success of an interdisciplinary team. This may involve providing training or professional development opportunities, as well as access to necessary resources and tools.

* * *

Conclusion

Managing an interdisciplinary team can be a challenge, but with careful planning and the right strategies in place, it is possible to build a strong, effective team that can drive innovation and success. By clearly defining roles and responsibilities, fostering open communication and collaboration, establishing a project management structure, and providing resources and support, businesses and organizations can ensure that their interdisciplinary AI teams are able to thrive and achieve their goals.

* * *

CHAPTER TWELVE

Working with external partners and vendors

As businesses and organizations increasingly turn to artificial intelligence (AI) to solve complex problems and drive innovation, they may need to work with external partners and vendors to access specialized skills, resources, or technologies. However, working with external partners and vendors can also introduce a range of challenges and considerations, including Identifying the right partners and vendors, Clearly defining the terms of the partnership or vendor relationship, Communicating effectively & Managing risks and challenges.

* * *

Identify the right partners and vendors

The first step in working with external partners and vendors is to identify the right individuals or companies to work with. This may involve evaluating their skills and expertise, as well as their track record and reputation. It is also important to consider factors such as compatibility with the company culture and values, as well as the potential risks and challenges of working with a particular partner or vendor.

* * *

Clearly define the terms of the partnership or vendor relationship

Once the partners or vendors have been identified, it is important to clearly define the terms of the partnership or vendor relationship. This may involve establishing contracts or agreements that outline the roles and responsibilities of each party, as well as any financial or legal considerations. * * * Communicate effectively Effective communication is critical to the success of any partnership or vendor relationship. It is important to establish clear lines of communication and ensure that all parties are on the same page in terms of goals, expectations, and progress.

* * *

Manage risks and challenges

Working with external partners and vendors can introduce a range of risks and challenges, such as delays, misunderstandings, or disagreements. It is important to anticipate and manage these risks and challenges to ensure that the partnership or vendor relationship is successful.

* * *

Conclusion

Working with external partners and vendors can be a valuable way for businesses and organizations to access specialized skills, resources, or technologies. However, it is important to carefully consider the potential partners or vendors and establish clear terms and effective communication to ensure that the partnership or vendor relationship is successful. By anticipating and managing potential risks and challenges, businesses and organizations can maximize the benefits of working with external partners and vendors while minimizing any potential negative impacts.

* * *

Designing and developing an AI product

CHAPTER THIRTEEN

Defining the user experience and interface for the AI product

As artificial intelligence (AI) becomes increasingly prevalent in a wide range of products and services, it is important to carefully consider the user experience and interface (UX/UI) of these products. A well-designed UX/UI can enhance the usability and accessibility of the AI product, while a poorly designed one can hinder its adoption and effectiveness. Some key considerations in defining the UX/UI for an AI product include: Identifying the target audience, Defining the user journey, Considering usability and accessibility & Incorporating feedback and testing.

* * *

Identify the target audience

The first step in defining the UX/UI for an AI product is to identify the target audience. Understanding the specific demographics, needs, and preferences of the intended users will help inform the design and ensure that the product meets their needs. * * * Define the user journey Defining the user journey involves identifying the specific steps that the user will take to interact with the AI product, from discovering the product to completing a task or achieving a goal. Understanding the user journey will help inform the design of the UX/UI and ensure that it is intuitive and easy to use.

* * *

Consider usability and accessibility

Usability and accessibility are critical factors in the design of any AI product. It is important to consider the needs of different users, including those with disabilities, and ensure that the product is easy to use and understand.

* * *

Incorporate feedback and testing

Incorporating feedback and testing into the design process is critical to ensuring that the UX/UI of the AI product meets the needs of the intended users. This may involve gathering feedback from users during the design process, as well as conducting usability testing to identify and address any issues.

* * *

Examples of user experience and interface for AI products

Here are some examples of user experience and interface for AI products:

Chatbots - Chatbots are a popular example of AI products. They are often used for customer support and helpdesk. The user interface for chatbots is a chat window, where users can type their queries and the chatbot responds with relevant information. The user experience is conversational, as if the user is talking to a human.

Personal assistants - Personal assistants such as Siri, Alexa, and Google Assistant are AI products that help users with various tasks such as setting reminders, making phone calls, playing music, and more. The user interface is often a voice command, and the user experience is conversational and hands-free.

Recommendation engines - Recommendation engines such as those used by Netflix and Amazon are AI products that suggest products or content to users based on their previous behavior. The user interface is often a list of recommended items, and the user experience is personalized and tailored to the user's preferences.

Image Recognition Product - Image recognition product is an AI product that allows users to search for images based on visual content. The user interface is often a search bar or a camera icon, and the user experience is visual and interactive.

Predictive Analytics Product Predictive Analytics Product is an AI product that uses data to make predictions about future outcomes. The user interface is often a dashboard or a report, and the user experience is analytical and data-driven.

Fraud detection - Fraud detection is an AI product that identifies and prevents fraudulent transactions. The user interface is often a notification or an alert, and the user experience is secure and trustworthy.

Natural language processing Product - Natural language processing (NLP) Product is an AI product that allows computers to understand and interpret human language. The user interface for NLP could be a chat window, a voice command, or a form field where users can input their text. The user experience is conversational and intuitive.

Autonomous vehicles - Autonomous vehicles such as self-driving cars are AI products that use computer vision, machine learning, and other AI technologies to navigate roads and traffic. The user interface could be a dashboard or a touchscreen display where users can input their destination or adjust settings. The user experience is hands-free and convenient.

Health diagnostics - Health diagnostics is an AI product that uses machine learning to diagnose diseases or conditions. The user interface could be a mobile app or a web portal where users can input their symptoms or medical history. The user experience is personalized and potentially life-saving.

Speech recognition Product - Speech recognition Product is an AI product that allows computers to recognize and transcribe human speech. The user interface could be a microphone or a voice command, and the user experience is hands-free and convenient.

Virtual assistants - Virtual assistants such as Google Duplex or OpenAI's GPT-3 are AI products that use natural language processing and other AI technologies to assist users with various tasks. The user interface could be a chat window, a voice command, or a mobile app. The user experience is conversational and intuitive.

Smart home devices - Smart home devices such as smart speakers, thermostats, and door locks are AI products that use machine learning and other AI technologies to automate and personalize home functions. The user interface could be a mobile app or a voice command, and the user experience is convenient and personalized.

These are just a few more examples of user experience and interface for AI products. The key is to design a user experience that is intuitive, user-friendly, and tailored to the specific use case of the AI product.

* * *

Conclusion

Defining the UX/UI of an AI product is a critical step in the development process. By carefully considering the target audience, the user journey, usability and accessibility, and incorporating feedback and testing, businesses and developers can ensure that the AI product has a well-designed UX/UI that meets the needs of its users and enhances its effectiveness.

* * *

CHAPTER FOURTEEN

Prototyping and testing the AI product

Prototyping and testing are important steps in the process of developing and implementing an artificial intelligence (AI) product. Prototyping involves creating a preliminary version of the product to test and refine, while testing involves evaluating the product to ensure that it meets the desired specifications and performance standards. Some key considerations in prototyping and testing the AI product include: Defining the scope and goals of the AI product, Identifying the tools and resources needed for prototyping and testing, Creating a prototype & Conducting testing.

* * *

Define the scope and goals of the AI product

Before prototyping and testing the AI product, it is important to clearly define the scope and goals of the project. This may involve identifying the specific problem or opportunity that the product is intended to address, the target audience, and the specific features and functionality that the product will include. Understanding the scope and goals of the AI product will help inform the prototyping and testing process and ensure that it is focused and achievable.

* * *

Identify the tools and resources needed for prototyping and testing

In order to prototype and test the AI product, it may be necessary to use a range of tools and resources, such as data sets, software, or hardware. It is important to carefully consider the tools and resources that will be needed and ensure that they are available and appropriate for the project. * * * Create a prototype Creating a prototype of the AI product is an important step in the development process, as it allows the team to test and refine the product before it is fully developed. The prototype should be a realistic representation of the final product, but it does not need to include all of the features and functionality that the final product will have.

* * *

Conduct testing

Once the prototype has been created, it is important to conduct testing to evaluate the product and identify any issues or areas for improvement. This may involve using a range of testing methods, such as user testing, functional testing, or performance testing, to ensure that the product meets the desired specifications and performance standards.

* * *

Examples of prototyping and testing methods for AI products

Here are some examples of prototyping and testing the AI product:

Paper prototyping - Paper prototyping involves creating rough sketches of the AI product design on paper, then having users interact with these sketches as if they were a real product. This method is used to quickly test and iterate on product designs before investing in more complex and expensive prototypes.

To conduct a paper prototyping session, designers create paper mockups of the product and ask users to complete tasks using the mockups. Users provide feedback on the design and usability of the product, and designers use this feedback to make improvements to the design. This method is low-cost and low-fidelity, making it ideal for early-stage product development.

Wizard of Oz testing - Wizard of Oz testing involves a human operator pretending to be the AI system and interacting with users. This method is useful for testing the user experience and interface before the AI system is fully developed.

To conduct a Wizard of Oz test, designers recruit users and have them interact with the product, believing that they are interacting with the AI system. A human operator behind the scenes responds to user input and provides the illusion of an AI system. This method allows designers to test the user experience and interface without investing in a fully functioning AI system.

MVP prototyping - MVP (minimum viable product) prototyping involves building a basic version of the AI product and testing it with a small group of users. This method is used to validate the product idea and identify key features and functions before investing in a more complex and expensive product development process.

To conduct an MVP prototyping session, designers build a basic version of the product and test it with a small group of users. These users provide feedback on the product, and designers use this feedback to identify key features and functions that should be included in the final product.

A/B testing - A/B testing involves testing two versions of the AI product with different groups of users to determine which version performs better. This method is used to optimize the user experience and interface for maximum effectiveness and engagement.

To conduct an A/B test, designers create two versions of the product and test them with different groups of users. The performance of each version is tracked, and the version that performs better is selected for further development.

Usability testing - Usability testing involves asking users to complete tasks using the AI product while being observed by researchers. This method is used to identify usability issues and make improvements to the user experience and interface.

To conduct a usability test, researchers recruit users and ask them to complete tasks using the AI product while being observed by researchers. Researchers take notes on the user's behavior and feedback, and designers use this feedback to make improvements to the user experience and interface.

Alpha and beta testing - Alpha testing involves testing the AI product internally by developers to identify bugs and performance issues. Beta testing involves testing the AI product by a small group of external users to gather feedback on the user experience and interface. These methods are used to improve the product before it is released to the public.

To conduct alpha testing, developers test the product internally to identify bugs and performance issues. They use this feedback to make improvements to the product. Beta testing involves testing the product with a small group of external users. These users provide feedback on the user experience and interface, and designers use this feedback to make final improvements before releasing the product to the public. These are some detailed examples of prototyping and testing methods for AI products. The key is to choose the right method based on the stage of development and the specific needs of the product.

* * *

Conclusion

Prototyping and testing are critical steps in the process of developing and implementing an AI product. By carefully considering the scope and goals of the project, identifying the tools and resources needed, creating a prototype, and conducting testing, businesses and developers can ensure that the AI product is effective and meets the needs of its users.

* * *

CHAPTER FIFTEEN

Building and integrating the AI product

Once the prototyping and testing phase is complete, the next step in the process of developing and implementing an artificial intelligence (AI) product is to build and integrate the final version of the product. This involves a range of activities and considerations, including Finalizing the design and architecture, Developing and implementing the AI solution, Integrating the AI product into existing systems and processes & Conducting final testing and validation.

* * *

Finalize the design and architecture

Before building and integrating the AI product, it is important to finalize the design and architecture of the product. This may involve refining the user experience and interface (UX/UI), as well as the underlying technical architecture and infrastructure of the product.

* * *

Develop and implement the AI solution

Developing and implementing the AI solution involves creating the necessary machine learning models and algorithms, as well as any additional software or hardware components that are required. It is important to carefully plan and coordinate the development process to ensure that the product is delivered on time and within budget.

* * *

Integrate the AI product into existing systems and processes

In many cases, the AI product will need to be integrated into existing systems and processes. This may involve integrating with other software or hardware systems, as well as adapting existing processes to accommodate the AI product. It is important to carefully plan and coordinate the integration process to minimize disruption and ensure a smooth transition.

* * *

Conduct final testing and validation

Before releasing the AI product, it is important to conduct final testing and validation to ensure that it meets the desired specifications and performance standards. This may involve conducting additional user testing, functional testing, or performance testing to identify and address any issues.

* * *

Examples of building and integrating AI products

Here are some examples of building and integrating AI products:

Building a chatbot - A chatbot is an AI product that uses natural language processing and machine learning algorithms to simulate human conversation. To build a chatbot, you would need to collect and preprocess data, train machine learning models to understand natural language, and develop a conversational interface that integrates with other systems or applications.

Integrating a chatbot into a customer service platform - A chatbot can be integrated into a customer service platform to provide automated support to customers. The chatbot can answer frequently asked questions, provide product recommendations, and direct customers to live support agents when necessary.

Building a recommendation system - A recommendation system is an AI product that uses machine learning algorithms to analyze user data and make personalized recommendations. To build a recommendation system, you would need to collect and preprocess data, train machine learning models to analyze user behavior, and develop an integration mechanism that allows the system to deliver recommendations to users.

Integrating a recommendation system into an e-commerce platform - A recommendation system can be integrated into an e-commerce platform to provide personalized product recommendations to users. The system can analyze user behavior and purchase history to suggest products that the user is likely to be interested in.

Building a fraud detection system - A fraud detection system is an AI product that uses machine learning algorithms to detect and prevent fraudulent transactions. To build a fraud detection system, you would need to collect and preprocess data, train machine learning models to identify patterns and anomalies in transaction data, and develop an integration mechanism that allows the system to communicate with other systems or applications.

Integrating a fraud detection system into a payment processing platform - A fraud detection system can be integrated into a payment processing platform to detect and prevent fraudulent transactions. The system can analyze transaction data in real-time and flag transactions that appear suspicious.

Building an autonomous vehicle - An autonomous vehicle is an AI product that uses sensors, machine learning algorithms, and decision-making systems to navigate roads and avoid obstacles. To build an autonomous vehicle, you would need to collect and preprocess data, train machine learning models to recognize and respond to different road conditions, and develop an integration mechanism that allows the vehicle to interact with other systems and sensors.

Integrating an autonomous vehicle into a transportation network - An autonomous vehicle can be integrated into a transportation network to provide efficient and safe transportation services. The vehicle can communicate with other vehicles and sensors in the network to navigate roads and avoid obstacles.

Building a medical diagnosis tool - A medical diagnosis tool is an AI product that uses machine learning algorithms to analyze patient data and assist with diagnosis and treatment recommendations. To build a medical diagnosis tool, you would need to collect and preprocess patient data, train machine learning models to recognize patterns and identify potential diagnoses, and develop an integration mechanism that allows the tool to communicate with healthcare professionals and other systems.

Integrating a medical diagnosis tool into a healthcare platform - A medical diagnosis tool can be integrated into a healthcare platform to assist healthcare professionals with diagnosis and treatment recommendations. The tool can analyze patient data and suggest potential diagnoses and treatments that the healthcare professional can review and consider.

* * *

Conclusion

Building and integrating an AI product is a complex and multifaceted process that requires careful planning and coordination. By finalizing the design and architecture, developing and implementing the AI solution, integrating the product into existing systems and processes, and conducting final testing and validation, businesses and developers can ensure that the AI product is delivered successfully and meets the needs of its users.

* * *

Launching and marketing an AI product

CHAPTER SIXTEEN

Developing a launch plan for the AI product

Developing a launch plan for an artificial intelligence (AI) product is an important step in bringing your product to market. A well-crafted launch plan can help you effectively introduce your product to the market, generate buzz, and drive adoption. Here are some key considerations for developing a launch plan for your AI product: Define your target market, Determine your marketing and promotion strategies, Plan your product launch event, Develop a timeline and budget & Monitor and measure results.

* * *

Define your target market

The first step in developing a launch plan is to clearly define your target market. This includes identifying the specific needs and challenges that your product is designed to address, as well as the demographics and preferences of your potential customers. By understanding your target market, you can tailor your launch plan to the right audience and ensure that your product is positioned for success.

* * *

Determine your marketing and promotion strategies

Once you have a clear understanding of your target market, the next step is to develop a plan for marketing and promoting your product. This includes identifying the channels and tactics you will use to reach potential customers, such as social media, paid advertising, content marketing, or public relations. You should also consider how you will differentiate your product from competitors and highlight its unique features and benefits to potential customers.

* * *

Plan your product launch event

A product launch event is a key component of any launch plan, as it provides an opportunity to showcase your product to the media, industry influencers, and potential customers. When planning your launch event, consider the location, format, and timing, as well as the attendees you want to invite. You should also plan the content and messaging for the event, including demos, case studies, and other materials that will help educate attendees about your product.

* * *

Develop a timeline and budget

A successful launch plan requires careful planning and execution, so it is important to develop a timeline and budget that outlines the key milestones and resources required to bring your product to market. This should include tasks like product development, marketing and promotion, and sales and distribution. By setting clear goals and allocating resources accordingly, you can ensure that your launch plan is well-executed and on track to achieve your desired outcomes.

* * *

Monitor and measure results

Finally, it is important to monitor and measure the results of your launch plan to determine its effectiveness. This includes tracking key metrics such as sales, customer engagement, and media coverage, as well as soliciting feedback from customers and industry experts. By regularly reviewing and analyzing these metrics, you can identify areas for improvement and make adjustments to your launch plan as needed.

* * *

Examples of AI products and their respective launch plans

Here are a few examples of AI products and their respective launch plans:

Chatbot for Customer Support:

Product Description:

A chatbot designed to handle customer queries, complaints, and support requests for a specific industry.

Launch Plan:

1. Identify the target market and customer needs for the industry.

2. Develop a comprehensive list of common queries and complaints for the industry.

3. Use natural language processing and machine learning algorithms to train the chatbot to handle these queries and complaints.

4. Test the chatbot with a small group of beta users to gather feedback and fine-tune the responses.

5. Launch the chatbot on the company website and social media channels, and promote it to existing customers through email campaigns and newsletters.

Personalized Recommendation Engine:

Product Description:

An AI-powered recommendation engine that suggests products based on the user's past purchase history and preferences.

Launch Plan:

1. Identify the target market and the types of products that would be suitable for personalized recommendations.

2. Collect data on past purchases and user preferences to train the recommendation engine.

3. Develop an intuitive user interface to showcase the recommended products.

4. Test the recommendation engine with a small group of beta users to gather feedback and fine-tune the recommendations.

5. Launch the recommendation engine on the company website and social media channels, and promote it to existing customers through email campaigns and targeted ads.

Autonomous Delivery Robot:

Product Description:

An AI-powered delivery robot that can navigate streets and deliver packages without human intervention.

Launch Plan:

1. Identify the target market and the types of products that would be suitable for autonomous delivery.

2. Develop a prototype of the delivery robot and test it in controlled environments.

3. Use machine learning algorithms to train the robot to navigate streets and avoid obstacles.

4. Test the robot in real-world scenarios with a small group of beta users to gather feedback and fine-tune the navigation.

5. Launch the delivery robot in a limited geographic area and gradually expand the coverage based on customer demand and feedback. Promote the launch through press releases, social media, and targeted ads.

* * *

Conclusion

In conclusion, developing a launch plan for an AI product requires careful planning and execution. By defining your target market, determining your marketing and promotion strategies, planning your product launch event, developing a timeline and budget, and monitoring and measuring results, you can effectively introduce your product to the market and drive adoption.

CHAPTER SEVENTEEN

Marketing and promoting the AI product

Marketing and promoting an artificial intelligence (AI) product can be a challenging task, as it requires a deep understanding of the technology and the target market. However, with the right strategies and tactics, it is possible to effectively showcase the benefits and value of your AI product to potential customers and drive adoption. Here are some key considerations for marketing and promoting an AI product: Understand your target market, Highlight the unique features and benefits of your product, Leverage social media and other online channels, Create high-quality content & Collaborate with partners and influencers.

* * *

Understand your target market

The first step in marketing and promoting your AI product is to have a clear understanding of your target market. This includes identifying the specific needs and challenges that your product is designed to address, as well as the potential benefits it offers. It is also important to understand the demographics, preferences, and buying habits of your target customers, as this will help you tailor your marketing efforts to the right audience.

* * *

Highlight the unique features and benefits of your product

To effectively market and promote your AI product, you need to clearly articulate its unique features and benefits. This includes highlighting the ways in which your product is different from other AI solutions on the market, as well as the specific problems it is designed to solve. Be sure to focus on the value your product provides to customers, rather than simply listing its technical features.

* * *

Leverage social media and other online channels

In today's digital age, social media and other online channels are essential tools for marketing and promoting any product, including AI products. By leveraging platforms like Twitter, LinkedIn, and Facebook, you can reach a wide audience and generate buzz around your product. In addition to social media, consider using other online channels like email marketing, blogs, and online communities to connect with potential customers and build a following.

* * *

Create high-quality content

In order to effectively market and promote your AI product, you need to create high-quality content that showcases its value and benefits. This can include case studies, demos, video tutorials, and other types of content that demonstrate the product in action. By creating engaging and informative content, you can educate potential customers about your product and its capabilities, which can help drive adoption and sales.

* * *

Collaborate with partners and influencers

Another effective strategy for marketing and promoting your AI product is to collaborate with partners and influencers in your industry. This can include working with other companies or individuals who have a strong following in your target market, as they can help amplify your message and reach a larger audience. Collaborating with partners and influencers can also help you tap into new networks and gain valuable insights into the needs and challenges of your target customers.

* * *

Examples of AI products and general marketing and promotion strategies that could be used for them

Here are some examples of AI products and general marketing and promotion strategies that could be used for them:

Chatbots: Chatbots are AI-powered virtual assistants that can communicate with customers through chat.

Marketing strategies for chatbots could include social media campaigns that highlight the benefits of using a chatbot, email campaigns that promote the chatbot's ability to answer customer questions, and trade show demonstrations of the chatbot's capabilities.

Personalized Recommendations: AI-powered personalized recommendation engines can analyze customer data to suggest products or services that customers are likely to be interested in.

Marketing strategies for personalized recommendations could include social media campaigns that highlight the benefits of using the recommendation engine, email campaigns that promote the engine's ability to make personalized recommendations, and trade show demonstrations of the engine's capabilities.

Predictive Analytics: Predictive analytics uses AI to analyze data and forecast future outcomes.

Marketing strategies for predictive analytics could include case studies and whitepapers that demonstrate the effectiveness of the technology, webinars that educate potential customers on the benefits of using predictive analytics, and trade show presentations that showcase the technology's capabilities.

Voice Assistants: AI-powered voice assistants like Amazon's Alexa or Google Assistant can perform a variety of tasks and answer questions for users.

Marketing strategies for voice assistants could include advertising campaigns that highlight the convenience of using a voice assistant, email campaigns that promote the assistant's ability to perform tasks hands-free, and trade show demonstrations of the assistant's capabilities.

Fraud Detection: AI-powered fraud detection systems can analyze data to detect fraudulent behavior.

Marketing strategies for fraud detection could include case studies and whitepapers that demonstrate the effectiveness of the technology, webinars that educate potential customers on the benefits of using fraud detection, and trade show presentations that showcase the technology's capabilities.

* * *

Conclusion

In conclusion, marketing and promoting an AI product requires a well-planned and strategic approach. By understanding your target market, highlighting the unique features and benefits of your product, leveraging social media and other online channels, creating high-quality content, and collaborating with partners and influencers, you can effectively showcase the value of your AI product and drive adoption.

* * *

CHAPTER EIGHTEEN

Gathering and analyzing customer feedback

Gathering and analyzing customer feedback is an essential part of any business, as it helps companies understand the needs, preferences, and satisfaction levels of their customers. This is especially important for artificial intelligence (AI) products, as customer feedback can provide valuable insights into how the product is being used and whether it is meeting the needs of its users. Here are some key considerations for gathering and analyzing customer feedback: Determine your objectives, Choose the right method for gathering feedback, Analyze the feedback, Communicate and act on the feedback & Monitor and track progress.

* * *

Determine your objectives

The first step in gathering and analyzing customer feedback is to determine your objectives. What do you want to learn from your customers, and how will this information help you improve your product or business? By setting clear objectives, you can focus your efforts and ensure that you are gathering the right type of feedback for your needs.

* * *

Choose the right method for gathering feedback

There are many different methods for gathering customer feedback, including online surveys, phone or email interviews, focus groups, and in-person interviews. The right method for your business will depend on your target audience, the type of feedback you are seeking, and your resources.

* * *

Analyze the feedback

Once you have gathered customer feedback, the next step is to analyze the data. This may involve coding the feedback into categories, calculating averages or percentages, and identifying patterns or trends. By analyzing the data, you can gain a deeper understanding of your customers‘ needs, preferences, and satisfaction levels, and use this information to inform your product development and business strategy.

* * *

Communicate and act on the feedback

It is important to not only gather and analyze customer feedback, but also to communicate and act on the feedback you receive. This may involve sharing the results with your team or other stakeholders, as well as implementing changes or improvements based on the feedback you receive. By demonstrating to customers that you are listening to their needs and taking action based on their feedback, you can build trust and strengthen your relationship with them.

* * *

Monitor and track progress

Finally, it is important to monitor and track the progress of any changes or improvements you make based on customer feedback. This can help you measure the impact of your efforts and identify areas for further improvement. By regularly gathering and analyzing customer feedback and taking action based on the insights you receive, you can continually improve your product or service and better meet the needs of your customers.

* * *

Examples of AI products that have acted on customer feedback and improved

Here are a few examples of AI products that have acted on customer feedback and improved:

Spotify: Spotify is a music streaming platform that has implemented AI algorithms to suggest music based on users' listening habits. The company also uses feedback from users to improve its recommendations, ensuring that the suggestions are relevant and useful.

Amazon: Amazon's Alexa is a popular virtual assistant that is powered by AI. Amazon has collected feedback from users to improve the voice recognition capabilities of Alexa, making it easier for users to communicate with the virtual assistant and get the desired results.

Netflix: Netflix is a video streaming platform that uses AI algorithms to suggest movies and TV shows to users. The company collects feedback from users on the recommendations and adjusts its algorithms to provide more accurate suggestions.

Grammarly: Grammarly is an AI-powered writing assistant that helps users write grammatically correct and clear sentences. The company uses feedback from users to improve its suggestions, ensuring that the writing assistant is useful and relevant to users.

Google: Google's search engine is powered by AI algorithms that help users find the information they need quickly and easily. Google collects feedback from users on search results and uses the feedback to improve its algorithms, ensuring that users get the most relevant and useful information.

Apple Siri: Apple's virtual assistant Siri is powered by AI and collects feedback from users to improve its natural language processing capabilities. Siri has been developed to understand the nuances of various accents, dialects, and languages.

Facebook: Facebook's newsfeed algorithm is powered by AI, and the platform uses feedback from users to improve the relevancy and accuracy of the newsfeed. Facebook also uses AI to identify and remove harmful content, such as hate speech and fake news.

Waze: Waze is a navigation app that uses AI to provide real-time traffic updates to users. The app collects feedback from users on traffic conditions and uses the information to adjust its algorithms, ensuring that users get the most accurate and up-to-date information.

Dropbox: Dropbox is a cloud storage platform that uses AI to help users organize and search their files. The platform collects feedback from users on the functionality of the search feature and adjusts its algorithms to improve the search results.

IBM Watson: IBM Watson is a suite of AI-powered products that have been developed to help businesses improve their operations. Watson collects feedback from users to improve its machine learning capabilities, ensuring that the products are relevant and useful to businesses.

* * *

Conclusion

In conclusion, gathering and analyzing customer feedback is an important part of any business, and is particularly crucial for AI products. By determining your objectives, choosing the right method for gathering feedback, analyzing the data, communicating and acting on the feedback, and monitoring and tracking progress, you can gain valuable insights into the needs and preferences of your customers and use this information to improve your product or business.

* * *

Growing and scaling an AI product

CHAPTER NINETEEN

Identifying and prioritizing new features and improvements

Identifying and prioritizing new features and improvements for an artificial intelligence (AI) product is a crucial part of product development and management. By regularly identifying and prioritizing new features and improvements, you can ensure that your product stays relevant and meets the evolving needs of your customers. Here are some key considerations for identifying and prioritizing new features and improvements: Gather customer feedback, Analyze market trends, Prioritize based on value and feasibility, Involve key stakeholders & Review and update regularly.

* * *

Gather customer feedback

The first step in identifying and prioritizing new features and improvements is to gather customer feedback. This can be done through surveys, interviews, focus groups, or other methods, and should focus on understanding the needs, challenges, and pain points of your customers. By gathering customer feedback, you can identify areas where your product may be lacking or where there is room for improvement.

* * *

Analyze market trends

In addition to gathering customer feedback, it is also important to analyze market trends to identify emerging opportunities or changes in customer needs. This can include keeping an eye on competitors, monitoring industry news and events, and conducting market research to understand the current landscape and identify potential areas for innovation.

Here are a few examples of AI products that had to add new features due to market trends:

Zoom: Zoom is a video conferencing platform that saw a massive surge in usage during the COVID-19 pandemic. To meet the changing needs of users, Zoom had to add new features such as virtual backgrounds, noise suppression, and breakout rooms to enhance the user experience.

Instagram: Instagram is a social media platform that has added several AI-powered features to keep up with market trends. For example, the platform introduced the "Explore" tab, which uses AI to suggest content based on users' interests. Instagram also introduced "Reels," a short-form video feature, to compete with the popularity of

TikTok.

Google Meet: Google Meet is a video conferencing platform that had to add new features to compete with other popular video conferencing platforms such as Zoom and Microsoft Teams. Google Meet introduced AI-powered noise cancellation and hand-raising features to enhance the user experience.

Amazon Alexa: Amazon's virtual assistant Alexa had to add new features to keep up with the popularity of smart home devices. Alexa introduced the ability to control smart home devices such as lights, thermostats, and security systems through voice commands.

Apple Siri: Apple's virtual assistant Siri had to add new features to keep up with the popularity of voice assistants. Siri introduced new functionalities such as the ability to make reservations, order food, and play music through voice commands.

* * *

Prioritize based on value and feasibility

Once you have identified potential new features and improvements, the next step is to prioritize them based on their value and feasibility. This may involve ranking them based on their potential impact on the product or business, as well as the resources required to implement them. By prioritizing based on value and feasibility, you can ensure that you are focusing on the most important and achievable improvements first.

* * *

Involve key stakeholders

It is important to involve key stakeholders in the process of identifying and prioritizing new features and improvements. This may include product managers, developers, sales and marketing teams, and other relevant parties. By involving these stakeholders, you can ensure that you are considering the needs and perspectives of different parts of the business and getting input from a diverse range of sources.

* * *

Review and update regularly

Finally, it is important to review and update your list of new features and improvements on a regular basis. This can help ensure that you are continuously identifying and prioritizing new opportunities for innovation and staying ahead of market trends. By regularly reviewing and updating your list, you can ensure that your product remains relevant and meets the evolving needs of your customers.

* * *

Conclusion

In conclusion, identifying and prioritizing new features and improvements is an essential part of product development and management. By gathering customer feedback, analyzing market trends, prioritizing based on value and feasibility, involving key stakeholders, and reviewing and updating regularly, you can ensure that your product stays relevant and meets the needs of your customers.

* * *

CHAPTER TWENTY

Managing the AI product's growth and scale

Managing the growth and scale of an artificial intelligence (AI) product can be a challenging task, as it requires a combination of technical expertise, business strategy, and customer focus. However, with the right approach, it is possible to effectively manage the growth and scale of your AI product and ensure its long-term success. Here are some key considerations for managing the growth and scale of an AI product: Develop a roadmap, Invest in infrastructure, Build a strong team, Foster customer relationships & Monitor and measure performance.

* * *

Develop a roadmap

The first step in managing the growth and scale of your AI product is to develop a roadmap that outlines your vision for the product and the key milestones and goals you want to achieve. This should include both short-term and long-term objectives, and should be based on a thorough understanding of your target market and the needs of your customers. A roadmap can help guide your product development efforts and ensure that you are focusing on the right priorities.

* * *

Invest in infrastructure

As your AI product grows and scales, it is important to invest in the infrastructure needed to support its growth. This may include things like data storage and processing capabilities, as well as the tools and systems needed to manage and maintain the product. By investing in the right infrastructure, you can ensure that your product has the resources it needs to function effectively and meet the needs of your customers.

* * *

Build a strong team

A strong and skilled team is crucial for managing the growth and scale of your AI product. This should include not only technical experts, but also business and customer-focused professionals who can help drive growth and success. By building a diverse and talented team, you can ensure that you have the right mix of skills and expertise to manage the product's growth and scale.

* * *

Foster customer relationships

Maintaining strong customer relationships is essential for managing the growth and scale of your AI product. This includes regularly soliciting and incorporating customer feedback, providing excellent customer support, and building trust and loyalty through your interactions with customers. By fostering strong customer relationships, you can ensure that your product meets the evolving needs of your customers and grows in a sustainable way.

* * *

Monitor and measure performance

Finally, it is important to regularly monitor and measure the performance of your AI product to ensure that it is meeting your growth and scale goals. This may involve tracking key metrics like adoption, usage, and customer satisfaction, as well as soliciting feedback from customers and industry experts. By regularly reviewing and analyzing these metrics, you can identify areas for improvement and make adjustments to your product as needed.

* * *

Examples of AI Products That Have Seen High Growth and Scale-Up

Here are a few examples of AI products that have seen high growth and scale-up:

Amazon Web Services (AWS): AWS is a cloud computing platform that uses AI to provide services such as machine learning, natural language processing, and speech recognition. AWS has seen tremendous growth in recent years, with revenues reaching over $40 billion in 2020.

Google Cloud Platform (GCP): GCP is a cloud computing platform that uses AI to provide services such as machine learning, natural language processing, and speech recognition. GCP has seen significant growth in recent years, with revenues reaching over $13 billion in 2020.

Salesforce Einstein: Salesforce Einstein is an AI-powered platform that helps businesses automate their sales, marketing, and customer service processes. Salesforce Einstein has seen rapid growth in recent years, with revenues reaching over $20 billion in 2020.

NVIDIA: NVIDIA is a technology company that specializes in graphics processing units (GPUs) for gaming, data centers, and artificial intelligence applications. NVIDIA's GPUs are used in AI applications such as computer vision, natural language processing, and autonomous vehicles. The company has seen significant growth in recent years, with revenues reaching over $16 billion in 2020.

UiPath: UiPath is an AI-powered platform that helps businesses automate their back-office processes, such as data entry and record-keeping. UiPath has seen rapid growth in recent years, with revenues reaching over $400 million in 2020. The company was also valued at over $35 billion in a recent funding round, making it one of the most valuable AI startups in the world.

IBM Watson: IBM Watson is an AI-powered platform that helps businesses improve their operations through machine learning, natural language processing, and other AI technologies. IBM Watson has seen significant growth in recent years, with revenues reaching over $4 billion in 2020.

Microsoft Azure: Microsoft Azure is a cloud computing platform that uses AI to provide services such as machine learning, natural language processing, and speech recognition. Microsoft Azure has seen significant growth in recent years, with revenues reaching over $59 billion in 2020.

Alibaba Cloud: Alibaba Cloud is a cloud computing platform that uses AI to provide services such as machine learning, natural language processing, and speech recognition. Alibaba Cloud has seen rapid growth in recent years, with revenues reaching over $8 billion in 2020.

OpenAI: OpenAI is an AI research organization that aims to create advanced AI technologies that benefit humanity. OpenAI has seen significant growth in recent years, with partnerships with major tech companies such as Microsoft and SpaceX.

DeepMind: DeepMind is an AI research organization that specializes in deep learning, a type of AI technology that enables machines to learn from data. DeepMind has seen significant growth in recent years, with notable achievements such as creating an AI system that can beat human players at the game of Go. The company was acquired by Google in 2015 and continues to be a leading player in the AI industry.

* * *

Conclusion

In conclusion, managing the growth and scale of an AI product requires a strategic and customer-focused approach. By developing a roadmap, investing in infrastructure, building a strong team, fostering customer relationships, and monitoring and measuring performance, you can effectively manage the growth and scale of your product and ensure its long-term success

* * *

CHAPTER TWENTY-ONE

Ensuring the AI product's continued success

Ensuring the continued success of an artificial intelligence (AI) product requires a combination of technical expertise, business strategy, and customer focus. By taking a proactive approach to product management and staying attuned to the needs and preferences of your customers, you can ensure that your AI product remains relevant and continues to drive value for your business. Here are some key considerations for ensuring the continued success of an AI product: Regularly gather and analyze customer feedback, Stay up to date on market trends, Invest in product development and innovation, Foster strong customer relationships & Monitor and measure performance.

* * *

Regularly gather and analyze customer feedback

One of the most important things you can do to ensure the continued success of your AI product is to regularly gather and analyze customer feedback. This can be done through surveys, interviews, focus groups, or other methods, and should focus on understanding the needs, challenges, and pain points of your customers. By regularly gathering and analyzing customer feedback, you can identify areas where your product may be lacking or where there is room for improvement, and take action to address these issues.

* * *

Stay up to date on market trends

To ensure the continued success of your AI product, it is important to stay up to date on market trends and the evolving needs of your customers. This may involve keeping an eye on competitors, monitoring industry news and events, and conducting market research to understand the current landscape and identify potential opportunities for innovation. By staying up to date on market trends, you can ensure that your product remains relevant and meets the evolving needs of your customers.

* * *

Invest in product development and innovation

Investing in product development and innovation is crucial for ensuring the continued success of your AI product. This may involve adding new features or capabilities, improving existing functionality, or developing new products or services that meet the needs of your customers. By regularly investing in product development and innovation, you can ensure that your product remains competitive and drives value for your business.

* * *

Foster strong customer relationships

Building strong and lasting customer relationships is essential for ensuring the continued success of your AI product. This includes providing excellent customer support, regularly soliciting and incorporating customer feedback, and building trust and loyalty through your interactions with customers. By fostering strong customer relationships, you can ensure that your product meets the evolving needs of your customers and drives long-term value for your business.

* * *

Monitor and measure performance

Finally, it is important to regularly monitor and measure the performance of your AI product to ensure that it is meeting your goals and driving value for your business. This may involve tracking key metrics like adoption, usage, and customer satisfaction, as well as soliciting feedback from customers and industry experts. By regularly reviewing and analyzing these metrics, you can identify areas for improvement and make adjustments to your product as needed.

* * *

Conclusion

In conclusion, ensuring the continued success of an AI product requires a proactive and customer-focused approach. By regularly gathering and analyzing customer feedback, staying up to date on market trends, investing in product development and innovation, fostering strong customer relationships, and monitoring and measuring performance, you can ensure that your product remains relevant and drives value for your business.

* * *

9 798890 022400

Printed by Libri Plureos GmbH in Hamburg,
Germany